TPR Storytelling
Student Book

ENGLISH YEAR 1
by
Todd McKay

Executive Editor
Dr. James J. Asher
Originator of the Total Physical Response
known worldwide as TPR

Published by
Sky Oaks Productions, Inc.
TPR World Headquarters Since 1973
P.O. Box 1102 • Los Gatos, CA 95031 USA
Phone: (408) 395-7600 • Fax: (408) 395-8440 • e-mail: tprworld@aol.com
web: www.tpr-world.com • Free TPR Catalog upon request.

TPR Storytelling
Student Book

ENGLISH YEAR 1

by

Todd McKay

Executive Editor
Dr. James J. Asher, Originator of TPR

Illustrated by
Gerard Arantowicz

ISBN 978-1-56018-026-5

—Order in English, Spanish, or French—

Published by
Sky Oaks Productions, Inc.
TPR World Headquarters Since 1973
P.O. Box 1102 • Los Gatos, CA 95031 USA

Phone: (408) 395-7600
Fax: (408) 395-8440
e-mail: tprworld@aol.com
Web: www.tpr-world.com

Free TPR Catalog upon request!

Order from our Full Color TPR Catalog by clicking on:
tpr-world.com

© Copyright 2000, 2013

All Rights Reserved Worldwide. No part of this publication may be reproduced for any purpose, *including classroom instruction* by any individual or institution, *including schools,* nor may it be stored in a retrieval system, or transmitted in any form or by any means: electronic, magnetic tape, mechanical, photocopying, recording or otherwise, without permission in writing from an executive officer of **Sky Oaks Productions, Inc.**

This book is protected internationally by the Universal Copyright Convention of Geneva, Switzerland.

TABLE OF CONTENTS
English - Year 1

Short Cartoon Stories #1

    1A. Hungry Dog 1

    1B. The Clumsy Dad 3

    1C. What a Trade! 5

    1D. He Speaks! 7

Everybody in now ready for ***Main Story 1 - Crunchy Salad*** 9

Short Cartoon Stories #2

    1A. A Quarter? 13

    1B. Don't Cut, Doctor! 15

    1C. Cry Baby 17

    1D. Crazy Choto 19

Everybody in now ready for ***Main Story 2 - Beware of Dog*** 21

Short Cartoon Stories #3

    1A. Let's Go To Chile! 25

    1B. Do You Ski in Colorado? 27

    1C. The Clown 29

    1D. Look Out! 31

Everybody in now ready for ***Main Story 3 - Dora Loves to Ski*** 33

The **Smith Family** 37

Vocabulary Sheet 38

Story 1A - Hungry Dog

Name _____

Date _____

Vocabulary

runs
looks
puts
buys

pieces
potatoes
goes
morning

Story - *Hungry Dog*

Eugene, a boy, _____ to the supermarket "Pueblo". It's 9:30 in the _____

_____ . He _____ salad, bread, and 25 _____. At home, he

_____ everything in the kitchen. The dog _____ to the table and

_____ at the bread. He eats 15 _____ of bread!

Cartoon Story 1A - *Hungry Dog*

PAGE 1

Another version:
_____
_____
_____
_____
_____
_____

Your version:

A	B
C	D

Your friend's version:

A	B
C	D

Cartoon Story 1A - *Hungry Dog*

Story 1B - The Clumsy Dad

Name _____

Date _____

A

B

C

D

Vocabulary

    making   reading
    sits   dining room
    puts   speaking

Story - *The Clumsy Dad*

Sara, a Cuban girl, is _____ a meat sandwich. She _____ the sandwich on a chair. Mom is _____ with Dad in the _____.

Dad enters the kitchen. He is _____ a small book. Oh my!

He _____ on the sandwich.

***Cartoon Story 1B** - The Clumsy Dad*
PAGE 3

Another version:

_____
_____
_____
_____
_____
_____

Your version:

| A | B |
| C | D |

Your friend's version:

| A | B |
| C | D |

Cartoon Story 1B - *The Clumsy Dad*

Story 1C - What A Trade!

Name _____

Date _____

Vocabulary

sells
feet
scarf
house

carries
looks at
money
large

Story - *What A Trade!*

There is a man that _____ flat bread. He is in front of the market. He has

_____ sandals on his _____. A woman _____ the flat

bread. She has no _____. She gives her pretty _____ to the man.

He _____ 45 flat breads to the woman's _____.

Cartoon Story 1C - What A Trade!

Another version:
_____
_____
_____
_____
_____
_____

Your version:

A	B
C	D

Your friend's version:

A	B
C	D

***Cartoon Story 1C** - What A Trade!*

Story 1D - He Speaks!

Name _____

Date _____

A

B

C

D

Vocabulary

    children
    eats
    rock
    ice cream

    walks
    speaks
    asks

Story - *He Speaks!*

There are two small _____ in the village. One is eating _____ and the other corn. He _____ 60 pieces of corn! Then a horse _____ through the village. He sits on a _____. "Where is the center of town?," _____ the horse. "He _____!," the children shout.

Cartoon Story 1D - He Speaks!

Another version:

_____
_____
_____
_____
_____
_____

Your version:

A	B
C	D

Your friend's version:

A	B
C	D

Cartoon Story 1D - *He Speaks!*

Name _____

Date _____

Main Story #1 - Crunchy Salad

> The dog's house is in the center of town. There are two big rocks and a potato in front of the house. The dog sets up a table in front of the house. He makes 51 sandwiches and puts them on top of the table. The dog sells the sandwiches quickly. He looks at the potato. The dog prepares a salad with the potato. A woman buys the potato salad. "There's a stone in my potato salad!", she shouts.

True or False

_____ 1. There is a market in front of the house.

_____ 2. Two rocks are in front of the house.

_____ 3. The house that has two rocks in front belongs to the dog.

_____ 4. The dog puts a rock in front of the town plaza.

_____ 5. The dog makes a lot of sandwiches.

_____ 6. The dog puts the sandwiches under the table.

_____ 7. Dad looks at the sandwiches.

_____ 8. A girl buys the potato salad.

_____ 9. There is a rock in the woman's salad.

_____ 10. The woman shouts.

Correct the above incorrect sentences in writing below.

_____

_____

_____

_____

_____

_____

Main Story #1 - Crunchy Salad

Name _____
Date _____

Questions:

1. Whose house is it?

2. What is in front of the house?

3. What is the dog doing?

4. Why is the woman shouting?

Questions for a classmate: Write in your classmate's answer:
Who?, Where?, How many?, How?

1.	
2.	
3.	
4.	

Listen…

A   B   C

Listening Activity:

1. ____   4. ____   7. ____   10. ____
2. ____   5. ____   8. ____   11. ____
3. ____   6. ____   9. ____   12. ____

Main Story 1 - Crunchy Salad

Main Story #1 - Crunchy Salad

Name _____

Date _____

Vocabulary

buys	front	puts	sets up	there's
center	house	quickly	shouts	with
dog's	potato	rocks	table	

Complete with the appropriate words.

The _____ house is in the _____ of town. There are two big _____ and a potato in _____ of the house. The dog _____ a table in front of the _____. He makes 51 sandwiches and _____ them on top of the _____. The dog sells the sandwiches _____. He looks at the _____. The dog prepares a salad _____ the potato. A woman _____ the potato salad. "_____ a stone in my potato salad!", she _____.

Invent another story:

_____

_____

_____

_____

_____

_____

Main Story #1 - Crunchy Salad

Name _____

Date _____

Make cartoon drawings of your story...

Write a summary of the Main Story

_____

_____

_____

_____

_____

_____

_____

_____

Story 2A - A Quarter?

Name _____

Date _____

Vocabulary

bag
eggs

hungry
market
pays

removes
slowly

Story - *A Quarter?*

At the _____, an old woman puts some Ritz crackers in her _____. She also puts 3 apples and _____ in the bag. She _____ $11 at the cash register. At 2:15 she is _____. She buys a burrito and eats it _____. She _____ 25¢ from the burrito!

Cartoon Story 2A - *A Quarter?*

Another version:

_____
_____
_____
_____
_____
_____
_____

Your version:

A	B
C	D

Your friend's version:

A	B
C	D

Cartoon Story 2A - A Quarter?

Story 2B - Don't Cut, Doctor!

Name _____

Date _____

Vocabulary

butter	he	November
coupons	is	soup
cuts	needs	

Story - *Don't Cut, Doctor!*

It _____ December 20th. Doctor Cortes _____ to buy groceries. _____ takes the newspaper and looks at the _____. He finds one for _____. It is 75¢. He finds another for vegetable _____. It is 50¢. He _____ all the coupons. But it is the newspaper from _____ 20th!

Another version:

_____
_____
_____
_____
_____

Your version:

A	B
C	D

Your friend's version:

A	B
C	D

Cartoon Story 2B - *Don't Cut, Doctor!*

Story 2C - Crybaby

Name _____

Date _____

Vocabulary

bread	English	hungry
cheese	everything	trips
cries	floor	

Story - *Crybaby*

Thomas, an _____ boy, is going to the supermarket. He is very _____.

He looks for the _____, ice cream, and ham. He puts _____ in his basket.

He _____ on the _____. Everything spills on the _____. Thomas _____ and cries.

Cartoon Story 2C - Crybaby

Another version:
_____
_____
_____
_____
_____
_____
_____

Your version:

A	B
C	D

Your friend's version:

A	B
C	D

Cartoon Story 2C - *Crybaby*

PAGE 18

Story 2D - Crazy Choto

Name _____

Date _____

Vocabulary

and　　　　　　　going　　　　　　　spills
blue　　　　　　　grabs　　　　　　　throw
crashes

Story - *Crazy Choto*

At 9:30, Choto _____ Theresa are _____ to the park. Theresa removes 3 balls. They are _____ in color, _____ in color, and white. She _____ the red one. Choto runs and _____ the ball. Watch out! He _____ with a girl and _____ her lemonade.

Another version:
_____
_____
_____
_____
_____
_____

Your version:

A	B
C	D

Your friend's version:

A	B
C	D

Cartoon Story 2D - *Crazy Choto*

Name _____

Date _____

Main Story #2 - Beware of Dog!

> An old man and his dog go to a huge market. They need apples, lemonade, and eggs. The dog is hungry. He finds an ice cream on the floor. He eats all the ice cream. There's is a little girl at the cash register. The old man looks at the girl. She looks at the dog. "Dogs are prohibited in the market!", the girl shouts. The girl grabs the dog and puts him in a big basket. The man slowly takes out $35. He pays the girl for the food. The dog cries.

True or False

_____ 1. It is a small market.

_____ 2. The dog is with a big boy.

_____ 3. They need lemonade and apples.

_____ 4. The old man is hungry and buys some sandwiches.

_____ 5. The dog eats the ice cream that's on the floor.

_____ 6. The ice cream is on the floor of the market.

_____ 7. The girl is at the cash register.

_____ 8. The dog looks at the man.

_____ 9. The girl puts the dog in the basket.

_____ 10. The dog removes $35 slowly.

Correct the above incorrect sentences in writing below.

_____

_____

_____

_____

_____

Main Story #2 - Beware of Dog!

Name _____

Date _____

Questions:

1. What is on the floor?

2. Who goes to the market?

3. Is there a boy in the box?

4. How does the man remove the money?

Questions for a classmate: Write in your classmate's answer:

Who?, Where?, How many?, How?

1.	
2.	
3.	
4.	

Listen…

A   B   C

Listening Activity:

1. ____   4. ____   7. ____   10. ____

2. ____   5. ____   8. ____   11. ____

3. ____   6. ____   9. ____   12. ____

Main Story #2 - Beware of Dog!

Name _____

Date _____

Vocabulary

big	for	grabs	lemonade	register
cries	girl	hungry	man	slowly
dog	go	is	market	
			on	

Complete with the appropriate words.

An old _____ and his dog _____ to a huge market. They need apples, _____, and eggs. The dog is _____. He finds an ice cream _____ the floor. He eats all the ice cream. There _____ a little girl at the cash _____. The old man looks at the _____. She looks at the _____. "Dogs are prohibited in the _____!", the girl shouts. The girl _____ the dog and puts him in a _____ basket. The man _____ takes out $35. He pays the girl _____ the food. The dog _____.

Invent another story:

_____

_____

_____

_____

_____

_____

Main Story #2 - Beware of Dog!

Name _____

Date _____

Make cartoon drawings of your story...

Write a summary of the Main Story

_____
_____
_____
_____
_____
_____
_____
_____
_____
_____

Story 3A - Let's Go To Chile!

Name _____

Date _____

Vocabulary

country	leaves	summer
home	puts on	turns
it	runs	

Story - *Let's Go To Chile!*

_____ is Sunday and Charles is at _____. It is _____ and it's hot. Charles sweats a lot. He _____ to the fan and _____ it on.

Now it is cool. Charles _____ skates quickly. He _____ the house.

He goes to another _____. He goes to Chile!

Another version:
_____
_____
_____
_____
_____
_____

Your version:

A	B
C	D

Your friend's version:

A	B
C	D

***Cartoon Story 3A** - Let's Go To Chile!*

Story 3B - Do You Ski in Colorado?

Name _____

Date _____

Vocabulary

chocolate	neighbor's	snowing
home	quickly	south
mountain	skis	

Story - *Do You Ski in Colorado?*

Geraldine _____ quickly in the _____ of Colorado. It is _____ a lot and it's windy. She falls and rolls down the _____. But there is Choto, the _____ dog. He gives hot _____ to Geraldine and she drinks it _____. Choto removes some skis and they ski _____.

Cartoon Story 3B - Do You Ski in Colorado?

Another version:
_____
_____
_____
_____
_____
_____

Your version:

A	B
C	D

Your friend's version:

A	B
C	D

***Cartoon Story 3B** - Do You Ski in Colorado?*

Story 3C - The Clown

Name _____

Date _____

A

B

C

D

Vocabulary

clown	her	shoes
has	paint	tall
hair	says	town square

Story - *The Clown*

Sarah and _____ friend Peter are going to the town square at 10:00. A ____ _____ man puts black _____ on his lips. He puts _____ paint on his cheeks. He puts large _____ on his feet. And he has a lot of green _____. "I don't understand," _____ Peter. "He is a _____," says Sarah.

Cartoon Story 3C - The Clown

Another version:

_____
_____
_____
_____
_____
_____

Your version:

A	B
C	D

Your friend's version:

A	B
C	D

Cartoon Story 3C - *The Clown*

Story 3D - Look Out!

Name _____

Date _____

Vocabulary

breaks	skiers	winter
hospital	tree	yellow
ski	vanilla	

Story - *Look Out!*

It is _____. Gerald and Doris _____ in the Colorado mountains. There are 45 _____. Gerald does not see the _____. He falls down and _____ his leg. Gerald goes to the hospital in a _____ ambulance.

He eats a lot of _____ ice cream in the _____.

Cartoon Story 3D - Look Out!

Another version:
_____
_____
_____
_____
_____
_____

Your version:

A	B
C	D

Your friend's version:

A	B
C	D

***Cartoon Story 3D** - Look Out!*

Name _____

Date _____

Main Story #3 - Dora loves to ski.

Peter, a tall man, has a house in the Pocono mountains. The house is green. There are many trees. During the summertime, Peter runs a lot and drinks lemonade. In the winter, it's really cold. He skiis with his friend Dora. She has big feet and black hair. Dora skiis very fast. She sweats a lot too. Now they are going home. Peter gives Dora hot chocolate but she drinks the lemonade. She takes off her big shoes. Oh no! Dora's feet are red!

True or False

_____ 1. Peter is a rather tall man.

_____ 2. Peter's house is in the Poconos.

_____ 3. The house is a red color.

_____ 4. Peter skis a lot in the summer.

_____ 5. He drinks lemonade and also runs.

_____ 6. In the Poconos, it's cool in the winter.

_____ 7. Peter's friend's name is Suzy.

_____ 8. His friend skis slowly because she has large feet.

_____ 9. Dora drinks hot chocolate because she likes it.

_____ 10. Dora has little red shoes.

Correct the above incorrect sentences in writing below.

_____

_____

_____

_____

_____

Main Story #3 - Dora Loves to Ski

Name _____
Date _____

Questions:

1. What is the tall man's name?

2. When do they ski?

3. What does Peter do in the summer?

4. What is Dora like?

Questions for a classmate: Write in your classmate's answer:
Who?, Where?, How many?, How?

1.	
2.	
3.	
4.	

Listen...

A	B	C

Listening Activity:

1. ____   4. ____   7. ____   10. ____
2. ____   5. ____   8. ____   11. ____
3. ____   6. ____   9. ____   12. ____

Main Story 3 - Dora Loves to Ski
PAGE 34

Main Story #3 - Dora Loves to Ski

Name _____

Date _____

Vocabulary

are	fast	home	in	runs
big	feet	hot	lemonade	tall
drinks	friend	house	many	too
			really	

Complete with the appropriate words.

Peter, a _____ man, has a house _____ the Pocono mountains. The _____ is green. There are _____ trees. During the summertime, Peter _____ a lot and drinks _____. In the winter, it's _____ cold. He skis with his _____ Dora. She has big _____ and black hair. Dora skis very _____. She sweats a lot _____. Now they are going _____. Peter gives Dora _____ chocolate but she _____ the lemonade. She takes off her _____ shoes. Oh no! Dora's feet _____ red!

Invent another story:

_____

_____

_____

_____

_____

_____

_____

Main Story #3 - Dora Loves to Ski

Name _____

Date _____

Make cartoon drawings of your story...

Write a summary of the Main Story

_____
_____
_____
_____
_____
_____
_____
_____
_____
_____

The Smith Family

Herman Smith — Rose Smith

- Dr. Smith — Olga Smith Miller — Peter Miller
  - Dora Miller
  - Gerald Miller
  - Charles Miller
- Teresa --- Thomas
- Professor Smith — Gertrude Smith
  - Eugene Smith
  - Sara Smith

The Smith Family

Vocabulary Sheet Number 1   Name

TPR PRODUCTS

**Books • Games
Student Kits
Teacher Kits
Audio Cassettes
Video Demonstrations**

Manufactured in the United States of America

Order directly from the publisher using your
<u>VISA</u>, <u>MASTERCARD</u>, or <u>DISCOVER CARD</u>
WE SHIP ASAP TO ANYWHERE IN THE WORLD!

Sky Oaks Productions, Inc.
Since 1973
P.O. Box 1102
Los Gatos, CA 95031 USA

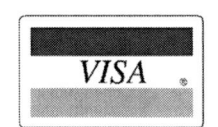

Phone: (408) 395-7600
Fax: (408) 395-8440
tprworld@aol.com

For fast service, order online:

www.tpr-world.com

Introduction
by the Originator of TPR,
Dr. James J. Asher

Dear Colleague,

If you are new to TPR, start with a solid understanding by reading my book, **Learning Another Language Through Actions** and Ramiro Garcia's **Instructor's Notebook: How to apply TPR for best results**.

To ensure success, pretest a few lessons before you enter your classroom. Try the lessons out with your children, your friends or your neighbors. In doing this, you

(a) become convinced that TPR actually works,

(b) build self-confidence in the approach, and

(c) smooth out your delivery.

For Students of All Ages, including Adults

Use TPR for new vocabulary and grammar, to help your students immediately understand the target language in chunks rather than word-by-word. This instant success is absolutely thrilling for students. You will hear them say to each other, "Wow! I actually understand what the instructor is saying."

After a "silent period" of about three weeks listening to you and following your directions in the target language (without translation), your students will be ready to talk, read and write. In our books, Ramiro and I will guide you step-by-step along the way.

Be sure to look through our online catalog at **www.tpr-world.com**. It's loaded with activities that will keep your students excited day after day as they move towards fluency in the target language.

Best wishes for continued success,

James J. Asher

The Latest from James J. Asher

**Award-winning Teacher, Researcher, and Writer;
Originator of the Total Physical Response™, known worldwide as TPR**

Learning Another Language Through Actions demonstrates step-by-step how to apply TPR to help children and adults acquire another language without stress.

- ✓ More than 150 hours of classroom-tested TPR lessons that can be adapted to teach any language.
- ✓ A behind-the-scenes look at how TPR was developed.
- ✓ Answers over 100 frequently asked questions about TPR.
- ✓ Easy to understand summary of 25 years of research with Dr. Asher's world famous Total Physical Response.

**Hot off the press!
7TH EDITION!
378 Exciting Pages**

Our best seller. (It's like sitting in the front row of a TPR workshop!)

Order #201

Learning Another Language Through Actions
by
James J. Asher
Originator of the
TOTAL PHYSICAL RESPONSE
known worldwide as
TPR
★ ★ ★ ★
Expanded 7th Edition!

New! *James J. Asher's*
Prize-Winning TPR Research

Order #7-CD

For the first time collected in one place on a CD, the complete prize-winning body of research by James J. Asher. Booklet available with the CD gives Asher's comments on each study with recommendations for future research. Saves you weeks of searching the internet or library.

- Shows step-by-step how Asher planned and successfully completed each research study.
- Includes all of Asher's pioneer studies in second language learning.

New! *James J. Asher's*
Brainstorming Kit

Transforms <u>ordinary</u> <u>committee</u> <u>meetings</u> into high-powered problem solving sessions!

Order #8

- Booklet and Transparencies with step-by-step directions to guide your brainstorming group.
- Helps your group understand what to do and why they are doing it.
- Discover options you never thought possible—and it's a lot of fun, too!

The latest books by James J. Asher

Brainswitching:
Learning on the Right Side of the Brain

| 2nd Ed. - 308 Pages | For *Fast*, *Stress-Free* *Access* to | Order #202 |

Languages, Mathematics, Science, and much, much more!

The Super School of the 21st Century

To help most students *learn anything fast*
on the right side of the student's brain,
in academics, sports, or technology!
Your students won't want to miss a single class!

Order #204

Stories about real people that excites kids about a career in science, mathematics, or technology!

Conversations with famous scientists and mathematicians

The Weird and Wonderful World of Mathematical Mysteries — Order #91

— AND —

Discoveries by Ordinary People that Changed the World — Order #2

For FL/ESL Students and Instructors
A Simplified Guide to Statistics:

Order #265

- How to evaluate the effectiveness of your instructional program to get the support you deserve from your organization.
- If you can do simple arithmetic, you will understand *every concept* in this easy-to-read book!
- Learn the ABC's of any first-class research program.

Added Bonus: Tips for organizing a successful master's thesis or doctoral dissertation!

Let's take a fresh look at Algebra!

Let's Make Sense of Algebra!
A fresh look at what algebra is all about.
Includes "Plato's Algebra" – the new, powerful algebra so simple, a child can understand!
James J. Asher, Ph.D.

Dedicated to...
- every person who ever found algebra baffling,
- parents struggling to help their kids with algebra homework, *and*
- teachers who work so hard trying to convince students that algebra is worthwhile.

New!

New discovery revealed in this book: Plato's Algebra

Order #4

So simple, a child can understand! So powerful, it could replace traditional algebra that we all endured in school.

This may be the most exciting discovery in the history of mathematics!

Students who drop out of school are not stupid.

They are smart enough to know that "school" is not meeting their needs. And you know what? The kids are right: The traditional school does not work for 1/3 to 1/2 of our students.

From the San Jose Mercury News, April 10, 2009:
"Kids dropping out of San Jose schools in just one year may go on to commit 534 violent crimes and suffer 200 million in lost wages over their lifetimes... according to a new study released Thursday... Statewide, for every three students who graduated high school in 2006-7, one dropped out..."

Let's turn it around. Let's make school relevant for all our kids:

The Super School of the 21st Century
by James J. Asher, Ph.D.

Table of Contents

Chapter 1: **Lessons to be learned from television commercials**

Chapter 2: **Reading**
The evidence: Children can learn to read and write before they enter the first grade, but most of us are slow-motion readers. How to accelerate reading so that the average student is able to read a book a day.

Chapter 3: **Mathematics**
Why math appears to be complex.
How to hook students with the Romance of Mathematics.

Chapter 4: **How to find the answer to any question**

Chapter 5: **Basic medicine**
The cost of medical treatment is too expensive for most people. The cost can be dramatically lowered if the average person knows some basics that answer the question: "Do I Really need to see a doctor?"

Chapter 6: **Basic law**
Most people cannot afford a lawyer.
With some basic information, the average person can answer this question, "Do I really need a lawyer or can I solve this problem myself?"

Chapter 7: **Nuts and Bolts**
Small appliance repair is a basic skill to rescue us from, "throw it away and buy a new one." The savings is in the billions and we will also save mountains of landfills.

Chapter 8: **The Art of Cooking**
With the revolution in relationships, this is a critical skill for boys and girls. Let's include nutrition.

Chapter 9: **The Intelligent Consumer**
A savvy consumer knows what to buy and what not to buy. How to manage money.

Chapter 10: **Lifetime Sports**
Football, baseball, and basketball are fun to watch and make money for schools. But, swimming, skiing, and hiking can be enjoyed by every student for a lifetime.

Chapter 11: **Relationships**
How to be comfortable with the opposite sex.
How to be a parent.

Chapter 12: **Music**
Kids with talent need some special attention.

Chapter 13: **Languages**
The traditional strategy of "Listen and repeat after me!" does not work for most students. It is enormous work with very meager gain.
We now know what does work for all students. So, there is no excuse not to graduate our kids fluent in three or four languages.

Chapter 14: **Summary**
Let's go! There is no time to waste!

The Super School of the 21st Century   Order #204
Order online: www.tpr-world.com

News Flash!

Discoveries by Ordinary People that Changed the World

by James J. Asher

Commentary by Albert Einstein

A fresh look at science, and technology in 25 exciting true stories such as:

- How two brothers, who own a bicycle shop in Ohio, build a bicycle that can fly.
- How penicillin is discovered when wind blows in some dirt from an open window.
- How an American student discovers the secret of DNA, and becomes the youngest person ever to win a Nobel Prize. His discovery transformed everyone's life in the 21st Century; yet amazingly, Harvard University tried to ban his personal story from publication.
- How a junior member of an Italian university discovers a simple equation that predicts the distance objects fall in space in seconds. A stunning discovery made even more remarkable when all he had to work with was a crude measure of time: water dripping from a bottle.
- How a fifteen year old boy discovers patterns of dots that enable blind people to read and write.
- How an uneducated janitor in London discovers simple patterns of electricity to enable giant turbines to move millions of gallons of water.
- How a young Englishman read about the principle of falling objects in space, adds one small detail, and discovers the jewel of mathematics, calculus, to predict how planets move around the sun. When you see that tiny detail, you will say, "Wow! So that is what calculus is all about!"

Order#	Title
2	Discoveries by Ordinary People that Changed the World

New!

I just completed a 263 page memoir about growing up in the 1930s, 40s, and 50s. I think you will have so much fun reading it you will want to start your own memoir today.

Comments from readers:

..."I started reading the book in bed and could not put it down."

..."I want several copies as gifts for friends."

..."I did not want the book to end."

..."The characters were so real, I felt I could reach out and touch them."

..."I remember reading **Catcher in the Rye** as a kid. This coming of age book is even better."

..."This is going to be a blockbuster of a motion picture."

After you read *Growing Up in Norman Rockwell's America*, please send me your comments!

James J. Asher

tprworld@aol.com

Growing Up in Norman Rockwell's America
A MEMOIR
James J. Asher

Order#	Title	
5	Growing Up in Norman Rockwell's America	263 pages

Captured for the first time on DVD!

The Northeastern Conference of FL/ESL instructors
Invited presentation by **Dr. James J. Asher**

New!

Dr. James J. Asher
Originator of TPR

Exciting 30 minute TPR demonstration in Arabic and Spanish followed by a lively Q&A session.

Narrated in English

Includes:

- How to stretch single words into hundreds of interesting sentences in any language.
- Your students will understand sentences, they have never heard before in the target language. This is the secret of fluency.
- Why it is <u>not</u> wise to tell your students, "Listen and repeat after me!"
- How to deal with adjectives.
- How to deal with grammar.

- How to make the transition from understanding to speaking, reading and writing.
- How to deal with abstractions.
- How to graduate your students with three or more languages.
- How to put your school on the map. Get ready for the Greyhound bus stopping at your school with teachers from around the world who want to take a look at your program.

Order Number: 104-DVD

Strategy for Second Language Learning

Your students can enjoy the thrill of achieving basic fluency in one or more languages if they remain in the program long enough. The problem is they "give up" too soon.

A solution

You will see adults of all ages from 17 to 60 understanding everything the instructor is saying in German. Within five minutes of the first class meeting, the faces of the adults reveal that they are convinced they can actually learn German.

After only a few weeks, students are ready to reverse roles and give directions in German. You will be entertained with their directions in German that have the instructor standing on a table and sitting in a corner. You will be impressed because you are witnessing the students actually thinking in the target language.

The grand climax

You will see the smooth transition from understanding German to speaking, reading, and writing within eight weeks. Time lapse photography will show you in 60 seconds, one student's progress through the entire course from zero understanding of German to conversational skill.

Show this video to your students

Instructors worldwide in all languages use this video to prepare their students to participate in the exciting TPR experience.

A bonus

As a bonus, we will include a copy of the original research article published in the *Modern Language Journal* that documents the significant achievement of the adults you will see in the video.

Strategy for Second Language Learning *(Order # 407-DVD)*

Produced by James J. Asher • DVD • Color • 19 minutes • Narrated in English

Dear Colleague:

Language instructors often say to me, "I tried the TPR lessons in your book and my students responded with great enthusiasm, but what can the students do **at their seats**?"

Here are effective TPR activities that students can perform **at their seats**. Each student has a kit in full color, such as the interior of a kitchen. Then you say in the target language, "Put the man in front of the sink." With your kit displayed so that it is clearly visible to the students, you place the man in the kitchen of your kit and your students follow by performing the same action in their kits.

As items are internalized, you can gradually discontinue the modeling. Eventually, you will utter a direction and the students will quickly respond without being shown what to do.

Each figure in the **TPR Student Kits** will stick to any location on the playboard **without glue**. Just press and the figure is on. It can be peeled off instantly and placed in a different location over and over.

You can create fresh sentences that give students practice in understanding hundreds of useful vocabulary items and grammatical structures. Also, students quickly acquire "function" words such as **up, down, on, off, under, over, next to, in front of,** and **behind**.

To guide you step-by-step I have written ten complete lessons for each kit (giving you about 200 commands for each kit design), and those lessons are now available in your choice of **English, Spanish, French, German,** or **Dutch**. The kits can be used with **children or adults** who are learning **any language** including **ESL** and the **sign language of the deaf**.

About the TPR Teacher Kits

Use the **transparencies** with an overhead projector to flash a playboard on a large screen. Your students **listen** to you utter a direction in the target language, **watch** you perform the action on the large screen, and then follow by performing the same action in their **Student Kits.**

Best wishes for continued success,

James J. Asher

P.S. My sister and I recently tried one of the Student Kits with a native speaker of Arabic giving directions. We were both surprised at how much vocabulary and grammar we picked up in only a few minutes of play.

Try this with any language you would like to acquire from Turkish to Chinese to Hebrew. It is simple, fast-moving, and it works!

Order No. 94

Total Physical Fun
by Jo Ann Olliphant

For language teachers at all levels who wish to enhance learning through the power of play!

- 100 Games field-tested with all ages from preschoolers to adults
- Students learn more easily when they are involved in interesting and entertaining activities
- For students at all levels learning any new language
- No special preparation necessary

Jo Ann Olliphant

Back By Popular Demand!

For every 5 Kits (Student or Teacher) in <u>any</u> assortment, select an additional kit of your choice as our **Free Gift** to you!

James J. Asher's TPR STUDENT KITS™

More than 300,000 Kits now being used in FL-ESL classes throughout the world!!

	ENGLISH Order Number	SPANISH Order Number	FRENCH Order Number	GERMAN Order Number	DUTCH Order Number
Airport ©	4E	4S	4F	4G	4D
Beach ©	12E	12S	12F	12G	12D
Classroom ©	10E	10S	10F	10G	10D
Garden ©	17E	17S	17F	17G	17D
Department Store ©	13E	13S	13F	13G	13D
Farm ©	60E	60S	60F	60G	60D
Gas Station ©	5E	5S	5F	5G	5D
Now Available ➤ Home ©	1E	1S	1F	1G	1D
Hospital ©	21E	21S	21F	21G	21D
Kitchen ©	2E	2S	2F	2G	2D
Main Street ©	15E	15S	15F	15G	15D
New ➤ Office ©	6E	6S	6F	6G	n/a

(Includes high tech business machines such as computers, cell phones, and even satellite communications!)

	ENGLISH	SPANISH	FRENCH	GERMAN	DUTCH
Picnic ©	16E	16S	16F	16G	16D
Playground ©	20E	20S	20F	20G	20D
Restaurant ©	40E	40S	40F	40G	40D
Supermarket ©	11E	11S	11F	11G	11D
Town ©	3E	3S	3F	3G	3D
United States Map ©	22E	22S	22F	n/a	n/a
New ➤ European Map ©	23E	23S	23F	23G	23D

(Recently updated to include the Middle East!)

4-KITS-IN-ONE: Community, School, Work, Leisure © 50E	50S	50F	50G	50D
Calendar © (limited supply) 31	(In English)			
TPR Student Kit Stories ©Uses vocabulary from the Student Kits.			Order Number 33	

TPR TEACHER KITS™
Transparencies for an <u>Overhead</u> Projector

	ENGLISH Order Number	SPANISH Order Number	FRENCH Order Number	GERMAN Order Number	DUTCH Order Number
Airport ©	4ET	4ST	4FT	4GT	4DT
Beach ©	12ET	12ST	12FT	12GT	12DT
Classroom ©	10ET	10ST	10FT	10GT	10DT
Garden ©	17ET	17ST	17FT	17GT	17DT
Dept. Store ©	13ET	13ST	13FT	13GT	13DT
Farm ©	60ET	60ST	60FT	60GT	60DT
Now Available ➤ Home ©	1ET	1ST	1FT	1GT	1DT
Hospital ©	21ET	21ST	21FT	21GT	21DT
Kitchen ©	2ET	2ST	2FT	2GT	2DT
Main Street ©	15ET	15ST	15FT	15GT	15DT
New ➤ Office ©	6ET	6ST	6FT	6GT	n/a
Picnic ©	16ET	16ST	16FT	16GT	16DT
Playground ©	20ET	20ST	20FT	20GT	20DT
Supermarket ©	11ET	11ST	11FT	11GT	11DT
Town ©	3ET	3ST	3FT	3GT	3DT
U.S. Map ©	22ET	22ST	22FT	n/a	n/a
New ➤ European Map ©	23ET	23ST	23FT	23GT	23DT

A Motivational Strategy for Language Learning

Produced by James J. Asher
DVD • Color • 25 minutes • Narrated in English

> The secret of a successful language program is to inspire students to continue year after year. This video will demonstrate how to motivate your students ages 17 to 60.

You will see that students are silent as they act in response to directions in Spanish starting with single words that expand within minutes into complex sentences. Notice the surprise on their faces as they realize they understand everything the instructor is saying in an alien language.

From understanding to speaking, reading, and writing

After several weeks, you will see that there comes a time when the students are ready to talk. This will happen spontaneously. They ask to reverse roles and give directions in Spanish to the instructor and classmates.

Next, you will see students, working in pairs, creating skits that are more entertaining than any stand-up comedian. Watch carefully because now you will see students actually thinking in the target language. You will also see a graceful transition to speaking, reading, and writing.

Show this video to your students

Instructors worldwide in all languages use this video to prepare their students to participate in the exciting TPR experience.

A bonus

As a bonus, we will include a copy of the original research article published in the *Modern Language Journal* that documents the stunning achievement of the students you will see in the video.

A Motivational Strategy for Language Learning
(Order # 406-DVD)
www.tpr-world.com

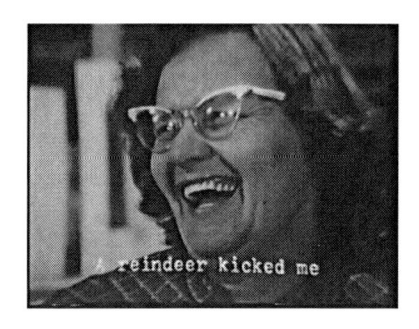

Children Learning Another Language: An Innovative Approach

Produced by James J. Asher
DVD • Color • 26 minutes • Narrated in English

If you are searching for other ways that motivate young people to acquire other languages, don't miss this demonstration with students in kindergarten through the 6th grade. The exciting ideas you will see can be applied in your classroom for any grade level and for any language including English as a second language.

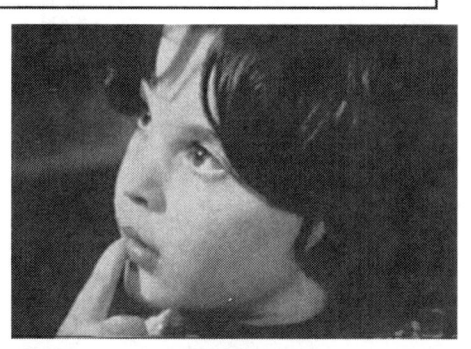

You will see young people...

- ✓ enjoying immediate understanding of everything the instructor is saying in Spanish or French.
- ✓ excited to be in the class day after day.
- ✓ spontaneously making the transition from understanding to speaking, reading, and writing.
- ✓ rapidly assimilating the target languages in chunks rather than word by word.

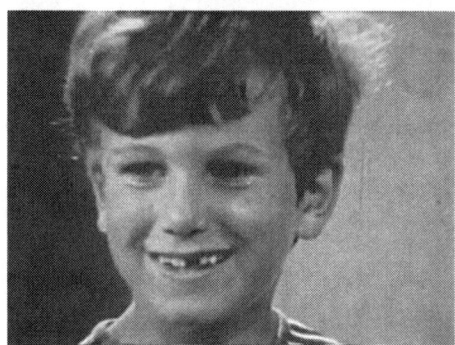

Be sure to show this video to your students

Use the video to prepare your students for the wonderful experience they are about to enjoy with TPR. The keen motivation and genuine achievement of these students will inspire parents, teachers and administrators at all levels.

A bonus

As a special bonus for you, we will include a complimentary copy of the original research published in *Child Development* that documents the extraordinary results you will see.

**Children Learning Another Language:
An innovative approach**

(Order # 435-DVD)

Order online: **www.tpr-world.com**

Demonstration of a New Strategy in Language Learning

Produced by James J. Asher
DVD • Black & White • 15 minutes • Narrated in English

This classic demonstration shows the complexity of spoken Japanese that American students can understand in only 20 minutes of TPR instruction. The Office of Naval Research was so impressed with this demonstration they awarded Dr. James J. Asher $50,000 to continue his ground-breaking research with the Total Physical Response, now known worldwide as TPR.

Shirou directs Hal Keely Jr. in Japanese to throw the toy car to him.

Retention after one year

You will be excited to witness the retention of the Japanese after one year. It is almost one-hundred percent.

Show this video to your students

Instructors worldwide in all languages use this video to prepare their students to participate in the exciting TPR experience.

A bonus

As a bonus, we will include a copy of the original research article published in the the *International Review of Applied Linguistics* that documents the significant achievement in Japanese of students like those you will see in the video.

Demonstration of a New Strategy in Language Learning
(Order # 408-DVD)
Order online: **www.tpr-world.com**

A powerful new tool for you, along with TPR and TPR Storytelling

Extra added attraction: Dr. James J. Asher explains what Tan-Gau is all about.

DVD • Black & White • 30 minutes • Narrated in English
Copyright 2009
Sky Oaks Productions, Inc.

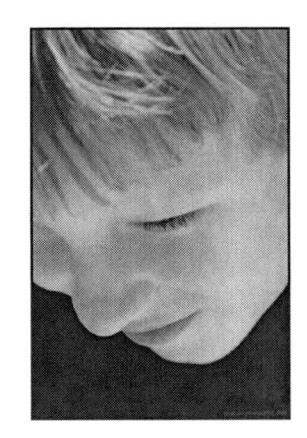

"Live" Demonstration of Tan-Gau

- ✓ In your very first meeting with your students, you experience immediate success.
- ✓ Every student is comfortable.
- ✓ Students have great fun deciphering what Raymond is saying in French.
- ✓ Every student understands what is happening. No one is ever left behind.

Something extra

In this extraordinary demonstration, the instructor, Raymond, speaking to the students in an alien language, allows the students to respond in their native language. This means that students are completely at ease and receptive to what Raymond is saying in French. Watch the expressions on the faces of these young students.

Remarkable results after five years in Canadian schools!

Middle of the first year
Most students are speaking French.
End of the second year
All students are conversing in French.

A bonus

The new tool that you have never seen before works for all languages and all ages, including adults.

"Live" **Demonstration of Tan-Gau!**
(Order # 9-DVD)
Order online: **www.tpr-world.com**

TPR Storytelling
by
Todd McKay

Outstanding Classroom Instructor
recently named to
Who's Who Among America's Teachers

- ✔ Pre-tested in the classroom for 8 years to guarantee success for your students.
- ✔ Easy to follow, step-by-step guidance each day for three school years - one year at a time.
- ✔ Todd shows you how to switch from activity to activity to keep the novelty alive for your students day after day.
- ✔ Evidence shows the approach works: Students in storytelling class outperformed students in the traditional ALM class.
- ✔ Each story comes illustrated with snazzy cartoons that appeal to students of all ages.
- ✔ There is continuity to the story line because the stories revolve around one family.
- ✔ Complete with tests to assess comprehension, speaking, reading and writing.
- ✔ Yes, cultural topics are included.
- ✔ Yes, stories include most of the content you will find in traditional textbooks including vocabulary and grammar.
- ✔ Yes, included is a brief refresher of classic TPR, by the originator— Dr. James J. Asher.
- ✔ Yes, games are included.
- ✔ Yes, your students will have the long-term retention you expect from TPR instructions.
- ✔ Yes, Todd includes his e-mail address to answer your questions if you get stuck along the way.
- ✔ Yes, you can order a video demonstration showing you step-by-step how to apply every feature in the Teacher's Guidebook.

Sky Oaks Productions, Inc.
P.O. Box 1102 • Los Gatos, CA, USA 95031
Phone: (408) 395-7600 • Fax: (408) 395-8440
e-mail: tprworld@aol.com
www.tpr—world.com
California residents: add sales tax. Prices subject to change without notice.

Use your VISA, MasterCard, or Discover Card to order from anywhere in the world!
WE SHIP ASAP!

Order Number	Title
400	Student Book - Year 1 **English**
401	Student Book - Year 2 **English**
402	Student Book - Year 3 **English**
410	Student Book - Year 1 **Spanish**
411	Student Book - Year 2 **Spanish**
412	Student Book - Year 3 **Spanish**
420	Student Book - Year 1 **French**
421	Student Book - Year 2 **French**
422	Student Book - Year 3 **French**
430	Complete Testing Packet for **English** Listening, Reading, Speaking, and Writing
431	Complete Testing Packet for **Spanish** Listening, Reading, Speaking, and Writing
432	Complete Testing Packet for **French** Listening, Reading, Speaking, and Writing
440	Teacher's Guidebook for **English**
441	Teacher's Guidebook for **Spanish**
442	Teacher's Guidebook for **French**
450	Transparencies for All Languages - Year 1
451	Transparencies for All Languages - Year 2
452	Transparencies for All Languages - Year 3

} Applies to Level 1, 2, 3

460	TPR Storytelling Video

Shows every step in the Teacher's Guidebook.

Exciting new products from Todd McKay!
TPR Index Cards
(Easy-to-handle 4x5 cards)

1. Index cards tell you exactly what to say, lesson by lesson.
2. 60 Cards with vocabulary from First Year textbooks.
3. When your students internalize this vocabulary, they're ready for a smooth transition to stories.
4. No need to fumble through a book.
5. No need to make up your own lessons.
6. Quick! Easy to use! Classroom-tested for success!
7. Works for students of all ages, including adults!

470	TPR Index Cards for **English**
471	TPR Index Cards for **Spanish**
472	TPR Index Cards for **French**
473	TPR Index Cards for **German**

TRIPLE EXPANDED 4TH EDITION!
BEST-SELLER!!

For 20 years, Ramiro Garcia has successfully applied the **Total Physical Response** in his high school and adult language classes.

Four NEW Chapters in the **Triple Expanded 4th Edition** (288 pages):
- **Speaking, Reading, and Writing**
- **How to Create Your Own TPR Lessons.**

More than **200 TPR scenarios** for **beginning** and **advanced students**.
- **TPR Games** for **all age groups**.
- **TPR Testing** for **all skills** including **oral proficiency**.

In this illustrated book, Ramiro shares the tips and tricks that he has discovered in using TPR with hundreds of students. No matter what language you teach, including **ESL** and the **sign language of the deaf**, you will enjoy this insightful and humorous book.

Instructor's Notebook: How to Apply TPR For Best Results By **RAMIRO GARCIA** Recipient of the **OUTSTANDING TEACHER AWARD**

Order #	Title:	Recommendation:
225	**Instructor's Notebook:** How to Apply TPR for Best Results	All Languages and All Ages
224	**Instructor's Notebook:** TPR Homework Exercises	Begin. & Interm. Students of All Ages
	Ramiro's brand-new companion book to the Instructor's Notebook!	All Languages

The Graphics Book
For Students of All Ages
by Ramiro Garcia
Recipient of the Most Remembered Teacher Award

Dear Colleague,

You recall that I introduced graphics in the **Instructor's Notebook: How To Apply TPR For Best Results.** Hundreds of teachers tried the *graphics* with their students in many different languages including ESL and were excited to discover that **students of all ages** thoroughly enjoyed working with the material.

Your students understand a huge chunk of the target language because you used **TPR**. Now, with my new *graphics* book, you can follow up with *300 drawings* on tear-out strips and sheets that help your students *zoom ahead* with **more vocabulary, grammar, talking, reading, and writing** in the target language. In this book, you will receive **step-by-step guidance** in how to apply the *graphics* effectively with **children and adults** acquiring **any** language, including ESL.

As an **extra bonus**, you will discover how to use the *graphics* to **test the achievement of your students** in comprehension, speaking, reading, and writing. In fact, I provide you with **60 multiple-choice graphic tests for beginning and intermediate students.**

Best wishes for continued success,

Ramiro Garcia

Available in English (228), Spanish (229), French (236), and German (237)

TPR BINGO©

TPR Bingo was created by **Ramiro Garcia**, author of the best-selling book, "Instructor's Notebook." In 30 years of applying the **Total Physical Response** in his high school and adult Spanish classes, **TPR Bingo** is the game that students want to play over and over.

TPR Bingo comes with complete **step-by-step directions** for playing the game, **rules for winning, 40 playboards** (one side for **beginners** and the reverse side for **advanced students**), a **master caller's board** with **100 pictures, chips,** and **caller-cards** in your choice of **English, Spanish, French** or **German**. As Ramiro says, "Try this game with your students. You will love it!"

Here's how **TPR Bingo** works: **You call out a direction in the target language** such as "The man opens the door." Students listen to the utterance, search for a matching picture and if it is on their playboard, cover it with a chip. Order the game in **English, Spanish, French** or **German**.

When students listen to the instructor utter directions in the target language, they are **internalizing comprehension**. But, as they advance in understanding, individual students will ask to play the role of the caller which gives students valuable practice in **reading and speaking.** Incidentally, as students play **TPR Bingo,** they **internalize numbers** in the target language from 1 through 100.

Available in English (226E), Spanish (226S), French (226F), and German (226G)

New! A TPR Language Classroom That Works for High-Speed Learning!

by award-winning language instructor,
Joan Christopherson

Order # 98

Dear Colleague,

At my high school, we were disappointed that only 30 percent of the students enrolled in either Spanish or French, and then student interest faded after one or two years.

We were determined to transform our foreign language offering into an award-winning program, but how to do it? Well, after many years of trial and error, my colleagues and I developed some very simple TPR Strategies that worked beautifully!

Result: The demand for foreign languages exploded so much that our school added Russian, Italian, German and Japanese! A remarkable turnaround for any school.

Now I would like to share these TPR Strategies with you. They are quick and simple, and easily adapted to any grade level, any language, and any instructor's teaching style.

For all languages and all ages!

Sincerely,
Joan

PS: James Asher's TPR always starts with fast-moving comprehension of the target language in chunks rather than word-by-word.

Host the team of James Asher and Todd McKay at your next FL/ESL Conference!

No Travelling - We Come To You! • Select a convenient time and place for Asher & McKay to demonstrate TPR and *authentic* TPR storytelling.

Dr. James J. Asher
tprworld@aol.com
World famous for his prize-winning research with the Total Physical Response, (TPR) for stress-free language learning. Featured speaker at several hundred workshops.

For a free quote, go to TPR-World.com

Todd McKay
thmckay1@aol.com
Outstanding classroom teacher and author of the successful student books: TPR Storytelling. Recently named to Who's Who Among America's Teachers.

TPR IS MORE THAN COMMANDS —*AT ALL LEVELS*

CONTEE SEELY & ELIZABETH ROMIJN
Winner of the Excellence in Teaching Award

Explodes myths about the Total Physical Response:

Myth 1: TPR is limited to commands.

Myth 2: TPR is only useful at the beginning of language acquisition.

Demonstrates how you can use Professor James Asher's approach—

✔ to *overcome problems* typically encountered in the use of TPR,

✔ to teach *tenses* and *verb forms* in *any language* in 6 ways,

✔ to teach *grammar, idioms,* and *fluent discourse* in a natural way, and

✔ to help your students *tell stories* that move them into fluent speaking, reading, and writing.

Shows you how to go from zero to correct spoken fluency with TPR.

Order #	Title:
95	TPR is More Than Commands All All Levels

Prize-Winning!
COMPREHENSION BASED LANGUAGE LESSONS
by Margaret S. Woodruff, Ph.D.

Here are **detailed lesson plans** for **60 hours** of **TPR Instruction** that make it **easy** for novice instructors to apply the **total physical response** approach **at any level.** The **TPR lessons** include

- **Step-by-step directions** so that instructors **in any foreign language** (including ESL) can apply comprehension training successfully.
- **Competency tests** to be given after the 10th and 30th lessons.
- **Pretested short exercises**—dozens of them to capture student interest.
- **Many photographs**

NOTE!
To satisfy everyone, we have printed the lessons in two languages — **English** and **German**, but we have charged you only the cost of printing a single language.

Order #290

Winner of the Paul Pimsleur Award
(With Dr. Janet King Swaffar)
Illustrations and photographs
by Del Wieding

TOTAL PHYSICAL RESPONSE IN THE FIRST YEAR
By Dr. FRANCISCO L. CABELLO with William Denevan

Dear Colleague:

I want to share with you the **TPR Lessons** that my high school and college students have **thoroughly enjoyed** and **retained** for weeks—even months later. My book has…

- A step-by-step script with props to conduct each class.
- A command format that students thoroughly enjoy. (Students show their understanding of the spoken language by successfully carrying out the commands given to them by the instructor. **Production** is delayed until students are ready.)
- Grammar taught implicitly through the imperative.
- Tests to evaluate student achievement.
- Now in **English, Spanish,** or **French.**

Sincerely,

Francisco Cabello, Ph.D.

Hot off the press in your choice of English (#221), Spanish (#220), or French (#222)!

TPR for Students of All Ages!

For 30 years, "Listen & Perform" worked for students of all ages learning English in the Amazon - and it will work for your students too!

Order this popular Student Book in **ENGLISH**, **SPANISH** or **FRENCH**!

More than 150 exciting pages of stimulating **Total Physical Response** exercises such as:

drawing • pointing • touching • matching • moving people, places, and things

With the **Student Book** and companion **CD**, each of your students can perform alone at their desks or at home to move from understanding the target language to speaking, reading, and writing!

Professor Stephen M. Silvers

Order #	Title:	Recommendation:
271	**Teacher's Guidebook** for All Languages (in **English**)	
270	**Student Book** in **English** for Listen and Perform	
278	**Audio CD** in **English** for Listen and Perform	
272	**Audio Cassette** in **English** for Listen and Perform	**TPR Lessons for students at all levels.**
274	**Student Book** in **Spanish** for Listen and Perform	
278	**Audio CD** in **Spanish** for Listen and Perform	
276	**Audio Cassette** in **Spanish** for Listen and Perform	
275	**Student Book** in **French** for Listen and Perform	
278	**Audio CD** in **French** for Listen and Perform	
277	**Audio Cassette** in **French** for Listen and Perform	

TPR for Young Children!

- Marvelously **simple format**: Glance at a page and instantly move your students in a logical series of actions.
- **Initial screening test** tells you each student's skill.
- After each lesson, there is a **competency test** for each students.
- Recommended for **preschool**, **kindergarden**, and **elementary**.

LEARNING WITH MOVEMENTS by Nancy Márquez

TPR Total Physical Response

Order #	Title:
240	Learning With Movements - English
241	Learning With Movements - Spanish
242	Learning With Movements - French

How to TPR Grammar

For Beginning, Intermediate, and Advanced Students of All Ages!
Edited by William Denevan, Trainer of Foreign Language Teachers at Stanford University.

"TPR is fine for commands, but how can I use it with other grammatical features?"
Eric Schessler shows you how to apply **TPR** for stress-free acquisition of 50 grammatical features such as:

Abstract Nouns	Expletives	Past Continuous	Prepositions of Place	Singular/Plural Nouns
Adjectives	Future - to be going to	Past Perfect	Prepositions of Time	Subject Pronouns
Adverbs	Future - Will	Past tense of Be	Present Continuous	Tag Questions
Articles	Have - Present and Past	Possessive Case	Present Perfect	Verbs
Conjunctions	Interrogative Verb forms	and Of expressions	Simple Past	Wh - Questions
Demonstratives	Manipulatives	Possessive Pronouns	Simple Present	
	Object Pronouns			

Order #	Title:	Recommendation:
260	**English Grammar Through Actions** by Eric Schessler	**ESL Students of All Ages**
261	**Spanish Grammar Through Actions** by Eric Schessler	**Students of Spanish of All Ages**
262	**French Grammar Through Actions** by Eric Schessler	**Students of French of All Ages**

How to TPR Vocabulary!

- Giant 300 page resource book, alphabetized for quick look-up.
- Yes, includes *abstractions!*
- Yes, you will discover how to TPR 2,000 vocabulary items from Level 1 and Level 2 textbooks.

Look up the word...   How to TPR it

Where 1. Pedro, stand up and run to the door. Maria, sit **where** Pedro was sitting. 2. Write the name of the country **where** you were born. 3. Touch a student who's from a country **where** the people speak Spanish (French, English).

For all ages!   Order #273

The **Command Book**
How to TPR 2,000 Vocabulary Items in Any Language
by STEPHEN SILVERS

How to TPR Grammar!
For Beginning, Intermediate, and Advanced Students of All Ages!
Available for English (#260), Spanish (#261), and French (#262)!

"TPR is fine for commands, but how can I use it with other grammatical features?"

Eric Schessler shows you how to apply TPR for stress-free acquisition of 50 grammatical features such as:

Abstract Nouns	Expletives	Object Pronouns	Possessive Pronouns	Simple Present
Adjectives	Future - to be going to	Past Continuous	Prepositions of Place	Singular/Plural Nouns
Adverbs	Future - Will	Past Perfect	Prepositions of Time	Subject Pronouns
Articles	Have - Present and Past	Past tense of **Be**	Present Continuous	Tag Questions
Conjunctions	Interrogative Verb forms	Possessive Case	Present Perfect	Verbs
Demonstratives	Manipulatives	and **Of** expressions	Simple Past	Wh - Questions

---

FAVORITE GAMES FOR FL - ESL CLASSES

(For All Levels and All Languages)
by
Laura Ayala & Dr. Margaret Woodruff-Wieding

Order #291

Laura J. Ayala

Chapter 1: Introduction

Chapter 2: Getting Started with Games
- How to get students involved
- How the games were selected or invented.

Chapter 3: Game Learning Categories
- Alphabet and Spelling
- Changing Case
- Changing Tense
- Changing Voice
- Describing Actions
- Describing Objects

Chapter 3 (Cont.)
- Getting Acquainted
- Giving Commands
- Hearing and Pronouncing
- Statements & Questions
- Negating Sentences
- Numbers and Counting
- Parts of the Body and Grooming
- Plurals and Telling How Many
- Possessive Adjectives & Belonging
- Recognizing Related Words
- Telling Time
- Using Correct Word Order.

Chapter 4: Games by Technique
- Responding to Commands
- Guessing
- Simulating
- Listing
- Categorizing
- Associating
- Sequencing
- Matching

Chapter 5: Special Materials For Games
- Objects
- Authentic Props
- Pictures
- Cards
- Stories

Chapter 6: Bibliography

Look, I Can Talk!
Original Student Book for Level 1
in English, Spanish, French or German

Editor's Tip... For best results, TPR the concrete words that will appear in the story!

Step-by-step, Blaine Ray shows you how to tell a story with **physical actions**, then have your students *tell the story to each other* in their own words **using the target language**, then **act** it out, **write** it and **read** it. Each **Student Book for Level 1** comes in your choice of *English, Spanish, French* or *German* and has

- ✔ 12 main stories
- ✔ 24 additional action-packed picture stories
- ✔ Many options for retelling each story
- ✔ Reading and writing exercises galore.

Blaine *personally guarantees* that each of your students will eagerly tell stories in the target language by using the **Student Book**.

Follow the steps in the **Teacher's Guidebook** and then work story-by-story with easy-to-use **Overhead Transparencies**.

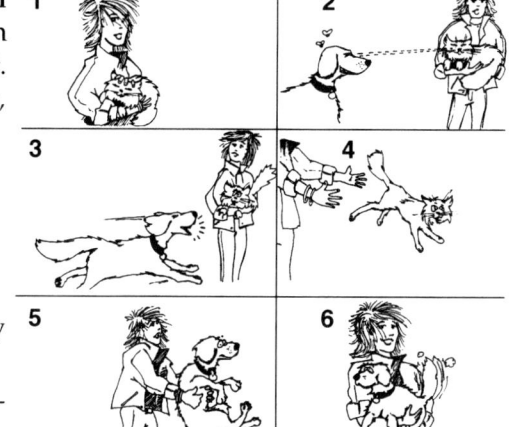

Order #	Title:
110	**Look, I Can Talk!** *Teacher's Guidebook for All Languages* (In English)
115	**Look, I Can Talk!** *Student Book for Level 1* - **English**
116	**Look, I Can Talk!** *Student Book for Level 1* - **Spanish**
117	**Look, I Can Talk!** *Student Book for Level 1* - **French**
118	**Look, I Can Talk!** *Student Book for Level 1* - **German**
111	**Look, I Can Talk!** *Overhead Transparencies for All Languages*

This is the original book that started TPRS!

Look, I Can Talk More!
Student Book for Level 2

by Blaine Ray with Joe Neilson, Dave Cline, Carole Stevens, and Christopher Taleck

Once again Blaine uses his exciting technique of blending **physical actions** with interesting story lines to get the students **talking**, **reading**, and **writing** in the **target language**. This second series of stories continues to build vocabulary while focusing on more advanced grammatical concepts common to second year language classes (i.e., use of infinitives, reflexive verbs, direct and indirect object pronouns, preterite vs. imperfect, etc.) Students enjoy using the target language to describe the stories as well as stories they have created.

Order #	Title::	
120	**Look, I Can Talk More!** *Student Book for Level 2* - **English**	**Level 2 ESL Students**
122	**Look, I Can Talk More!** *Student Book for Level 2* - **Spanish**	**Level 2 Spanish Students**
123	**Look, I Can Talk More!** *Student Book for Level 2* - **French**	**Level 2 French Students**
121	**Look, I Can Talk More!** *Student Book for Level 2* - **German**	**Level 2 German Students**
124	**Look, I Can Talk More!** *Overhead Transparencies for All Languages*	**To help you demonstrate 10 main stories**

LIVE ACTION
ENGLISH, SPANISH, FRENCH, GERMAN, ITALIAN, OR JAPANESE!!

Each page is a "happening" — a list of imperatives to be performed in the classroom with props. There are 67 happenings such as Washing Your Hands, Going Swimming, Using a Pay Phone, Taking Pictures, and Going to the Movies (Go to the movie theater. Buy a ticket. Give it to the ticket-taker at the door, etc.)

Excellent for all levels. Basic survival vocabulary can be used as a basis for a great variety of lessons, especially verb work.

Elizabeth Romijn and Contee Seely

Order #	Title:
255	Live Action **English**
227	Live Action **English** - Audio Cassettes
256	Live Action **Spanish**
257	Live Action **French**
258	Live Action **German**
259	Live Action **Italian**
226	Live Action **Japanese**

✓ FIND the products you want at www.tpr-world.com.
✓ WRITE on this Order Form or your School Purchase Order the items you want.
✓ FAX or MAIL the Order Form and/or School Purchase Order to us. We'll do the rest, pronto!

TPR ORDER FORM
BOOKS • VIDEO DEMONSTRATIONS • STUDENT KITS • GAMES

Sky Oaks Productions, Inc.
P.O. Box 1102 • Los Gatos, California, USA 95031
Since 1973

Phone: (408) 395-7600
e-mail: tprworld@aol.com
Fax: (408) 395-8440

Use your VISA, Discover, or MasterCard to order from anywhere in the world! WE SHIP ASAP!

Please Print or Type:

Name _____ Date of Order: _____

School *or* Residence _____

Street or P.O. Box _____ City _____ State _____ Zip _____

Country _____ Phone (___) _____ Fax (___) _____ E-mail _____
Please print.

MasterCard VISA

Discover Card, Visa/MC Card No. ☐☐☐☐ ☐☐☐☐ ☐☐☐☐ ☐☐☐☐

Expiration Date _____ Authorized Signature _____

PAGE	ORDER NO.	QUANTITY	DESCRIPTION & LANGUAGE	EACH	TOTAL

☐ Send <u>order form</u> only
☐ Send <u>complete catalog</u> plus <u>complimentary article</u>
☐ My <u>Check</u> or <u>Purchase Order</u> is enclosed.

Subtotal _____

California residents: Add sales tax _____

USA: Add 12% for shipping & handling (minimum: $6.95) _____

Outside USA: for S & H add 30% (minimum: $13.95) _____

P.S. To order <u>directly online</u>, go to **tpr-world.com**

Prices subject to change without notice.

(U.S. Currency) Total $ _____

Order Form